DK DIGITAL
Photography

Alan Buckingham

LONDON, NEW YORK,
MELBOURNE, MUNICH, AND DELHI

Produced for Dorling Kindersley Ltd by
Cooling Brown Ltd:
Creative Director Arthur Brown
Editor Kesta Desmond
Designer Tish Jones

For Dorling Kindersley Ltd:
Senior Editor Kitty Blount
Managing Editor Linda Esposito
Managing Art Editor Diane Thistlethwaite
Art Director Simon Webb
Publishing Managers Caroline Buckingham,
Andrew Macintyre
Category Publisher Jonathan Metcalf
Production Controller Luca Bazzoli
Picture Researcher Marie Ortu
DK Picture Library Sarah Mills
DTP Designer Natasha Lu
Jacket Editor Mariza O'Keeffe
Jacket Designer Chris Drew

Editorial consultant Chris George

First published in Great Britain in 2005 by
Dorling Kindersley Limited,
80 Strand, London WC2R 0RL
Copyright © 2005 Dorling Kindersley Limited
A Penguin Company

05 06 07 08 09 10 9 8 7 6 5 4 3 2 1

A CIP catalogue for this book is available from the
British Library.
ISBN 1405307110

Colour reproduction by Colourscan, Singapore
Printed in China by L-Rex

Discover more at
www.dk.com

Contents

Introduction

Digital photography is an amazing invention. Why? Because it has completely changed the way we take pictures. In the old days, when cameras used film, you waited for days, weeks, or even months before your photos were developed and printed and you got a chance to see the results. Of course, if you'd made a mistake or something had gone wrong, it was just too bad. There was no chance to re-shoot.

Digital cameras have done away with all that waiting. They're immediate. As soon as you've taken a picture, you can look at it on your camera's LCD screen and, if it's no good, delete it and take another one. In fact, you can take lots more – as many as you like. They're free.

Just as important is what you're able to do with your photos once you've taken them. Once they're copied onto your computer, you can really start having fun. Digital photography is creative and rewarding. This book contains lots of tips on how to take better pictures and ideas for what you can do with them. Once you've read it, it's up to you. So just get out and start shooting!

What's on the CD?

The CD contains software that lets you edit photos on a computer, as well as a selection of images you can use for all sorts of digital trickery.

Software

Adobe® Photoshop® Elements 3.0 is an image-editing application designed for amateur photographers. It contains all the tools you'll need to create images like those in Section 3 (Digital Trickery) and Section 4 (It's Showtime!). On the CD is a special free trial version of the software that lasts for 30 days.

Loading the software

The trial software should work on computers running either Microsoft Windows 2000 or XP and Apple Mac OSX v10.2.8 or v10.3. Insert the CD in your computer. An opening screen will appear with a short menu. Click on **What's on this CD**, then follow the instructions. On a Mac, double-click on **Digital_Photography**, then double-click on **Start_MAC**. An opening screen will appear. Follow the instructions as for PC above.

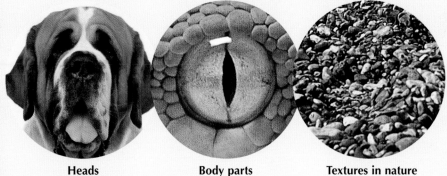

| Heads | Body parts | Textures in nature |

Image resources

On the CD you'll also find folders containing lots of images that you can use to create your own special photo effects. They include animal heads to swap with those of your friends, strange tongues, tails, eyes, and ears to make your family look even weirder, pictures of places from all over the world to use as exotic backgrounds, and some great textures for making your own picture frames.

1

Start here

Why is digital so great?

35-mm film

Digital photos cost nothing to shoot, can be copied without any loss in quality, and can be printed cheaply at home. They can be stored and manipulated on a computer, "burnt" onto CD or DVD, and sent anywhere round the world via email, mobile phone, or the Internet – easily and almost instantly.

35-mm slides

Instant pictures

For more than 100 years, cameras have used film. But film is expensive, difficult to handle, and can get scratched or dirty. Film must be developed and printed before you can see the results. With digital, you can take a picture and view it on your LCD screen straight away.

TECH TIP

What's a pixel?

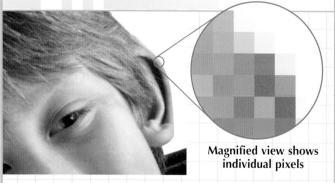

Magnified view shows individual pixels

A digital image is made up of a grid of tiny squares, each of which has its own level of brightness and its own particular colour. When you take a digital photo, the image sensor in your camera captures this information, which is then encoded digitally as a number made up of 0s and 1s. Each square in the picture grid is called a pixel.

Take a picture with your phone

Most mobile phones now have a built-in digital camera – the quality of which is getting better all the time. This means you can send photos to friends and family, from one phone to another, with incredible speed.

Transfer your photos to a computer

Taking digital photos is only the first step. Next, you can copy or "download" them from your camera to your computer. Software included free with most PCs and cameras will display your pictures on screen.

Have fun with your photos

With inexpensive image-editing software, you can start manipulating your pictures – fixing problems, changing colours, erasing details, combining shots, and applying crazy special effects.

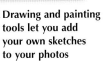

Drawing and painting tools let you add your own sketches to your photos

View and organize thumbnails of your photos on screen

Images from most digital cameras can be printed to fill an A4 sheet

Print your photos

Home printers now produce high-quality colour prints in just a few minutes, often direct from a memory card without the digital images going via a computer.

CD inserts with thumbnail pictures show the images on each disc

Publish your own photos online

Burn photos on CD

Images can be copied or "burnt" onto recordable CDs or DVDs, either for storage or as slideshows that you can view on a computer or television screen.

Share your photos

It's easy to send digital photos to your friends via email or to upload them on the Internet as a web photo gallery that you can invite anyone to log on to and look at.

Know your camera

Most digital cameras switch back and forth between two modes. One is for shooting – the image on the LCD screen is the shot the camera is about to take. The other mode is for playback – the LCD screen lets you scroll through and view the pictures you've shot.

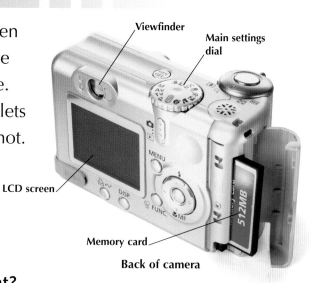

Viewfinder

Main settings dial

LCD screen

Memory card

Back of camera

Shutter button

On/off switch

Front of viewfinder

Flash

Zoom lens control

Zoom lens

Front of camera

What does what?

The most important controls – the on/off switch, the zoom lens control, and the shutter button, which you press to take a picture – should be easy to find. Others may be less obvious. Start by learning where to find flash on/off, the self-timer, and macro on/off (see p.32).

Camera icons

Standard graphical symbols are displayed on the LCD (liquid crystal display) screen to let you know which of the following shooting modes your camera is set to.

🌷 Macro   🕐 Self-timer

⚡ Flash on   ⚡ Flash off

🗗 Continuous 🎥 Movie

Memory cards

Digital cameras store the pictures you shoot in the form of digital data on a removable memory card or stick. From here they can easily be transferred to a computer or a printer, then the card can be erased and used again. Memory cards come in different shapes and sizes and can hold hundreds or in some cases thousands of images.

Loading a memory card into its camera slot

CompactFlash card

SD card

MemoryStick

Macro on and flash off

Shooting mode

Cool camera features

Manufacturers are packing more and more features into digital cameras. Here are the ones to look out for.

- Powerful optical zoom (see p.20).
- Macro setting – for taking really close-up shots.
- Movie mode – good fun, though not a replacement for a real video camera.
- Continuous burst mode – when the shutter is down, the camera keeps taking pictures.
- Long shutter settings – for taking pictures at night.
- Wide range of ISO adjustment – to make the camera's sensor more sensitive to light (see p.22).
- White balance control – to record colours accurately and counteract colour casts from artificial lights (see p.42).
- On-board special photo effects – including pictures in vivid colours, black-and-white, or sepia.

Shots in a movie sequence

Thumbnail images

Frame number and ready-to-transfer icon

09/90   10/90

11/90   12/90

Playback mode

Using the LCD screen

The LCD screen lets you review your photos. Navigate via small thumbnail images, then zoom in close to check focus, facial expressions, and other details. The LCD also displays menus for settings you'll use less often, such as date and time, image resolution, and ISO sensitivity.

TECH TIP

Megapixels

A megapixel is one million pixels. So, a six megapixel digital camera, for example, takes pictures each made up of six million pixels – they might be 3,000 pixels wide by 2,000 pixels high. The more pixels in your photo, the more you can enlarge it or crop in without losing quality.

Image made from 1,000,000 pixels

Image made from 10,000 pixels

Image made from 1,000 pixels

Go on... take a picture

Your digital camera is probably one that allows you simply to point, click, and take a picture. The camera will do all the hard work for you – measuring the amount of light and calculating the right exposure, and checking how far away your subject is in order to set the correct focus. All you need to do is hold your camera steady, frame your picture carefully, and start shooting.

Use your zoom or move closer to cut out wasted space from the picture

Hold the camera with two hands

Stand as still as you can and hold the camera steady

1 **Turn your camera on** If the flash is going to fire, make sure that you switch on red-eye reduction.

2 **Frame your shot** Zoom in and out to get the shot you want. The LCD screen usually gives you a better preview than the viewfinder.

3 **Press the shutter** Press halfway down to focus and to get a light reading, then all the way. Don't stab at the shutter or make jerky movements.

In playback mode, zoom in and scroll around the picture to check it is in sharp focus

2.0x   4.0x

4 **View the picture** Switch to playback mode and take a good look at the photo you've just taken. Are your subjects smiling? Are their eyes open? Are they looking at the camera?

Image slightly blurred

Poor composition – their heads are chopped off

Perfect picture – this is the one to keep

5 **Save or delete?** Be critical. Are you happy with the shot or not? If there's anything you don't like, take another one – it costs nothing, and nine times out of ten you'll never get another chance. Delete any shots that you know you don't want.

Picture quality

Digital cameras let you choose the quality or "resolution" of the pictures you take – and it's important what you select. Here's why.

Low resolution

High resolution

High or low resolution?

High-resolution images are made up of a lot of pixels, which means you can crop in on a small area and enlarge it without the pixels showing. These types of pictures take up a lot of room on your memory card.

Large or small pictures?

Low-resolution images contain fewer pixels, so they are useful if you're short of space on your memory card. And they're good for emailing or posting on the Internet. But you won't be able to print them out at large sizes without them looking blocky.

Low resolution = small picture

High resolution = large picture

Ten tips for better pictures

Anyone can take better photos. All you have to do is follow ten easy-to-remember tips. They're listed below, and then covered in more detail on the pages that follow. It also helps to really look at the picture you're about to take before you press the shutter. Would it be better to zoom in or out, move closer or farther away, step to the left or right, or crouch down to ground level? If everything looks fine, then go ahead and shoot!

✅ **Tip 1: Hold the camera still**

✅ **Tip 2: Focus on the right thing**

✅ **Tip 3: Think about composition**

✅ **Tip 4: Zoom in close...**

✅ **Tip 5: But don't get too close**

✅ **Tip 6: Make sure there's enough light**

✅ **Tip 7: Don't shoot into the light**

✅ **Tip 8: Check the background**

✅ **Tip 9: Beat shutter lag**

✅ **Tip 10: Shoot more not less**

What went wrong?

Do your photos look like these? If so, it's no surprise. What you see here are examples of some of the mistakes most frequently made by ordinary amateur photographers. Why did they turn out so badly? Usually, it's something really simple that can easily be avoided next time.

Poor composition
The girl on the left is almost out of the picture, and the girl in the middle has lost the top of her head. Better framing would have helped this shot.

Reflections When you shoot through glass, you may get a reflection of your own camera. Get up as close to the glass as you can, and turn your flash off.

Reflection of camera in glass

Flash turns iris from black to red

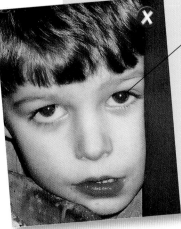

Red eye This is caused by your flash, and there's no easy solution to it. Some cameras have a red-eye reduction mode but, if that doesn't work, fix the problem later on your computer.

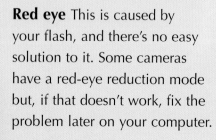

Shallow focus Although the llama's eyes are in focus, its nose and mouth are not. There's a limit to what will be sharp at telephoto settings like this. Try moving closer and zooming out to a wider angle.

Too far away This is a dull shot: the four figures are way off in the distance and we really can't see what's happening. It's a classic example of where it would have paid off to zoom in closer.

Out of focus because not in centre of frame

Camera shake This shot is blurred because the camera was moving as the picture was taken. At slow shutter speeds, you must hold the camera absolutely still or support it on something solid.

Wrong focus The camera's autofocus system has taken its distance reading from the middle of the frame instead of from the boys. Centre on one of them, use focus lock, then re-compose the picture.

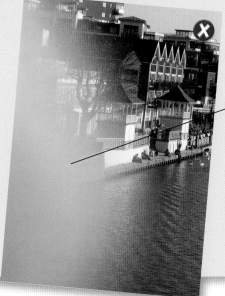

Finger in front of lens

Patterns caused by internal reflections within camera lens

Lens obstruction Make sure that you keep everything clear of the camera lens, and check before you shoot that neither your camera strap nor your own hand is blocking the view.

Lens flare Shooting directly into the sun can overexpose part of the picture and create patterns of circles, polygons, or streaks caused by reflections of light inside the lens. A lens hood can reduce flare.

1 Hold the camera still

Moving the camera while you take a picture almost always produces a blurred photo. It's perhaps the most common mistake of all. While the camera's shutter is open, you must keep it absolutely still in order to capture a pin-sharp image.

✗ A little bit shaky?

When the light is low, say in a wood or forest, your camera needs to keep its shutter open for longer in order to get a correct exposure, so you're more likely to get camera shake. If you can't use flash, perhaps because your subject is too far away, steady yourself or your camera against something solid.

Even slight camera shake creates a blur

Steady the camera for sharp photos

Rest your arms and hands on the ground

Use the viewfinder and steady the camera against your face

✓ Get a grip

There are a number of techniques for keeping your camera still while hand-holding it. Try resting your elbows on a table, a wall, or a car door. Sit cross-legged with your elbows on your knees, or lie face down with your arms resting on the ground. If you have to stand up, tuck your elbows in, breathe slowly and calmly, and press the shutter as you breathe out.

Keep your hands steady

Pull your upper arms tight into your body

Rest your elbows on a firm surface

Using a camera tripod

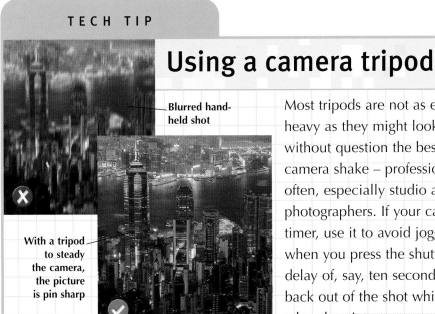

Blurred hand-held shot

With a tripod to steady the camera, the picture is pin sharp

Most tripods are not as expensive or as heavy as they might look. And they're without question the best way to avoid camera shake – professionals use them often, especially studio and landscape photographers. If your camera has a self-timer, use it to avoid jogging the camera when you press the shutter. Set up a time delay of, say, ten seconds, then stand back out of the shot while the camera takes the picture.

2 Focus on the right thing

It's unlikely that everything in your picture will be sharp. When objects close to the camera are in focus, things in the distance are usually blurred – and vice versa. This is called depth of field. Your camera usually focuses on what's in the middle of the frame; side objects that are closer or further away get blurred.

Here, the building in the background is in focus because it's in the centre. The girls are a lot nearer to the camera and are both out of focus.

1 Pre-focus Point at something in the frame that you want to be sharp, press the shutter halfway down, and hold it there to "lock" it.

2 Re-frame your shot Without taking your finger off the shutter button, re-compose your picture so that it's framed the way you want it. Now press the shutter all the way down.

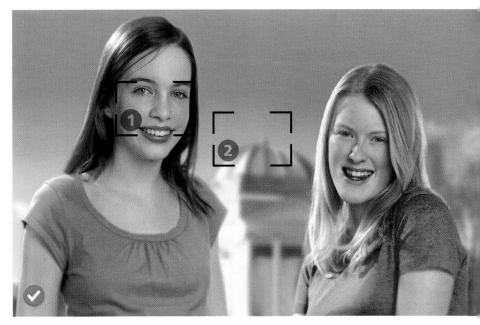

3 Think about composition

Composition is about what you decide to put in your picture and what you decide to leave out. Are you too far away? Or too close? And what can you see in the background? Composition is also about how you hold the camera (upright or at an angle) and which viewpoint you take. Are you head-on, off to one side, looking up, or looking down? The most important thing is to take a second or so to "see" your picture and check that you're happy with it before you press the shutter.

Upright format is often best for portraits

This symmetrical arrangement isn't very interesting

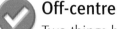

Choose a format

Don't be afraid to turn your camera on its side. Head-and-shoulder photos of people are often better shot in an upright or "portrait" format – yet it's amazing how many beginners shoot them as horizontal or "landscape" pictures.

❌ Bang in the middle

What's wrong with this picture? At first glance, not much perhaps. The boy is in the middle of the frame and he's nicely balanced by the two plants on either side. But in this case, the symmetry actually makes the photo a bit boring.

✅ Off-centre

Two things have changed here. First, we're much closer, so we can see the "tough-guy" expression on the boy's face. Second, he now appears slightly to one side of the picture, which makes the composition more interesting. Photographers often divide the frame into thirds in this way.

An interesting foreground

Photos of landscapes can be disappointing. They often look a lot less beautiful or dramatic than the subject itself. Making sure there's an object in the foreground will help to give landscape shots a feeling of size and distance.

Foreground objects add interest and a sense of scale

Doorways and arches can act as great natural frames

Diagonal lines

There is nothing in this picture other than rows of tulips, but it is such a strong composition that it can stand alone. Try to create similar abstract pictures yourself – using lines and patterns made by tree trunks, railings, or shadows.

Simple diagonal lines and just two colours make this a great composition

You've been framed

Our eyes are always drawn to a subject that's positioned within a frame of some kind. Windows and doors do the job perfectly, but you can also create frames by using the trunks and branches of trees.

Look up, look down

The usual advice given to photographers is to get up or down to the same level as the object you are photographing, but there's nothing wrong with breaking the rules from time to time. You can get great pictures by going for really unusual angles – try holding your camera up high and pointing it downwards, or lie on the ground and shoot upwards.

Hold your camera above your head

Capture a tree canopy by laying your camera flat on the ground

To get this sense of looking down, stand on a chair

4 Zoom in close...

Taking a picture from too far away is a common mistake, but one that is easy to avoid. Either use your zoom to fill the frame with your subject, or simply move in closer. You'll get much better photos if you lose boring background clutter and concentrate on what is really interesting.

1 Too far The girl is too far away, and there's too much road in the foreground and too many buildings and people in the background.

2 Zooming in closer This is better. The girl's blue dress and pink headdress now fill the frame, but the background is still cluttered and we can't see the expression on the girl's face.

Small details of the girl's costume become visible when you're really close

TECH TIP

What is digital zoom?

Many of today's digital cameras have both an optical zoom and a digital zoom.

Optical zooming is done by the lens moving in or out of the camera body and changing the angle of view, so that subjects are magnified.

Digital zooming is done by the camera's on-board processor. It selects just a part of the optical image and then enlarges it electronically. Although this can be useful, use it with care – the quality of the image worsens the more it's blown up. Your picture quality may be better if you simply move in closer.

Digital zoom can reveal blocky pixels

...or move closer

When you take a picture of a person, their face is often the most important thing. If you're too far away, you won't really capture their expression. So, if you can't zoom in, simply move closer.

Too far away

You don't need the boy's whole body or the bushes and fence in the background of this picture. It's just his face you want to see.

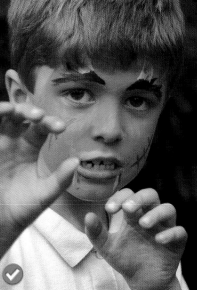

Move closer

Simply moving closer produces a better photo. It concentrates on the boy's grisly painted face, and also puts the distracting background nicely out of focus.

③ **Spot on!** We're close enough now to see the smile on the girl's face and to pick out the detail in her hair and clothes. At last, the picture has really come alive.

5 But don't get too close

If you get too close, your camera may not be able to focus properly. It may warn you of this, but it will still let you take the shot and you'll end up with a blurred picture. For really close-up shots, your camera may have a "macro" setting (see page 32).

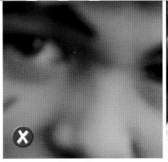

Too close

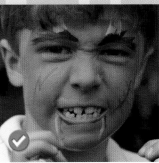

About right

6 Make sure there's enough light

Without sufficient light, your photo will be underexposed. Your camera's sensor won't be able to record a detailed image, and your picture will be dark. Most digital cameras automatically measure light levels and trigger the flash in low light. But the flash isn't always the best solution – in some cases you'll get better results by increasing the light sensitivity of your camera or by using a long exposure time and resting your camera on a firm surface.

The stage is still in darkness – it's too far away

Flash reaches figures close to the camera

Flash doesn't always help

The flash can light things up when it's too dark, but it only travels a certain distance. Even when your camera tells you it can take a picture, the flash may not illuminate what you actually want to see.

Completely black – you can't see anything!

Detail visible, even in the shadows

Just the right amount of light

Getting the exposure right is a balancing act: too much light and the photo will be overexposed; too little and it will be underexposed. It's easy to tell the difference: overexposed photos are pale and washed out, while underexposed photos are dark and gloomy.

TECH TIP

Adjusting sensitivity

One of the great things about many digital cameras is that you can increase the light sensitivity or "ISO" of the image sensor, enabling you to take pictures without a flash in low light. However, there's one thing to watch: photos taken at high ISO settings can reveal strange-coloured spots – called "noise" – when enlarged.

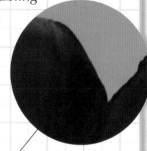

Low noise

Image at normal size

High noise

Flash on or off?

With flash

A close-up indoor shot like this will almost certainly cause the flash to go off. However, although the exposure may be correct, you may find that the bright flash produces a hard, bleached-out, unnatural look.

Without flash

If you turn off the flash, you'll get a warmer, more natural light. However, it's unlikely that you'll be able to hold the camera steady during the longer exposure time that's needed, so the photo may be blurred.

No flash – but camera supported

Here's the perfect solution: rest the camera on the table or use a tripod, so that it stays perfectly still. That way you should get a lovely candlelit picture that's pin sharp.

7 Don't shoot into the light

Scenes that contain a strong light source – such as the sun, a bright sky, or light shining through a window – can fool even the best automatic cameras. They tend to expose correctly for the brightest areas and underexpose everything else.

Underexposed
Here, the camera has taken its light reading from the bright desert sky and calculated the correct exposure time for it. But the camel and rider are so underexposed that they appear too dark.

Getting it right
If you must shoot into the light, set your camera so that the flash fires even though you're outdoors. This will illuminate the side of the camel and rider closest to you so that both they and the sky are correctly exposed.

8 Check the background

It's common to concentrate so hard on the main subject in a picture that you forget to look at what's going on in the background. This results in busy pictures that are full of clutter or classic mistakes such as TV aerials sprouting from people's heads.

✓ Learn to see everything
To avoid mistakes, slow down before you shoot. Take a moment to look carefully at everything in the frame before you go ahead and press the shutter. If there's something distracting in the background, try moving to one side, zoom in closer, or crouch down to get a low angle.

Pole sticking out of head

Background is too busy

✗ Classic mistakes
A cluttered, confusing background has spoiled one picture, and a telegraph pole is in an unfortunate position in the other.

9 Beat shutter lag

Automatic cameras do a lot of on-board processing, and there is often a time delay between pressing the shutter and the camera taking a picture. This is called "shutter lag".

The boy has played his stroke and the ball has moved out of the frame

✗ Too late!
By the time the shutter goes off, the action is over and you've missed the moment.

✓ How to cope with shutter lag
The trick is to think ahead and try to get your camera to do some of its processing work before you take your picture.

1 Get in position Use your zoom to frame the boy before the shot.

2 Half press the shutter
Keep your finger down to hold it there. Your camera will pre-focus on the boy and take a light reading to calculate the exposure.

3 Choose the moment
Press the shutter all the way down to take your picture. Don't move your camera until a few moments after the click.

Pre-focusing and anticipating the shot allows you to freeze just the right moment

10 Shoot more not less

Digital photos cost nothing to shoot, so don't hold back. Capturing just the right moment in a fast-paced action sequence or the perfect expression on a person's face is a hit-and-miss affair. So aim to take as many shots as you can, then delete the ones you don't want later on.

One person looking away

Not ready yet

Still talking and laughing

At last... everyone looks their best

The best of the bunch

Group shots like this can be really difficult to get right. It's a rare moment when everyone in the picture is smiling, has their eyes open, and is looking at the camera. You'll find that just when three people look perfect, the fourth blinks, giggles, sneezes, or looks away. The only answer is to take lots of pictures and then select the best one.

TECH TIP

Continuous shooting

Many digital cameras can shoot a brief series of pictures one after the other in a single burst. The camera will keep taking pictures for as long as you hold down the shutter button. You may need to use a lower quality setting, but continuous shooting is still a useful technique for capturing fast-moving subjects such as this girl dancing.

2

What shall I photograph?

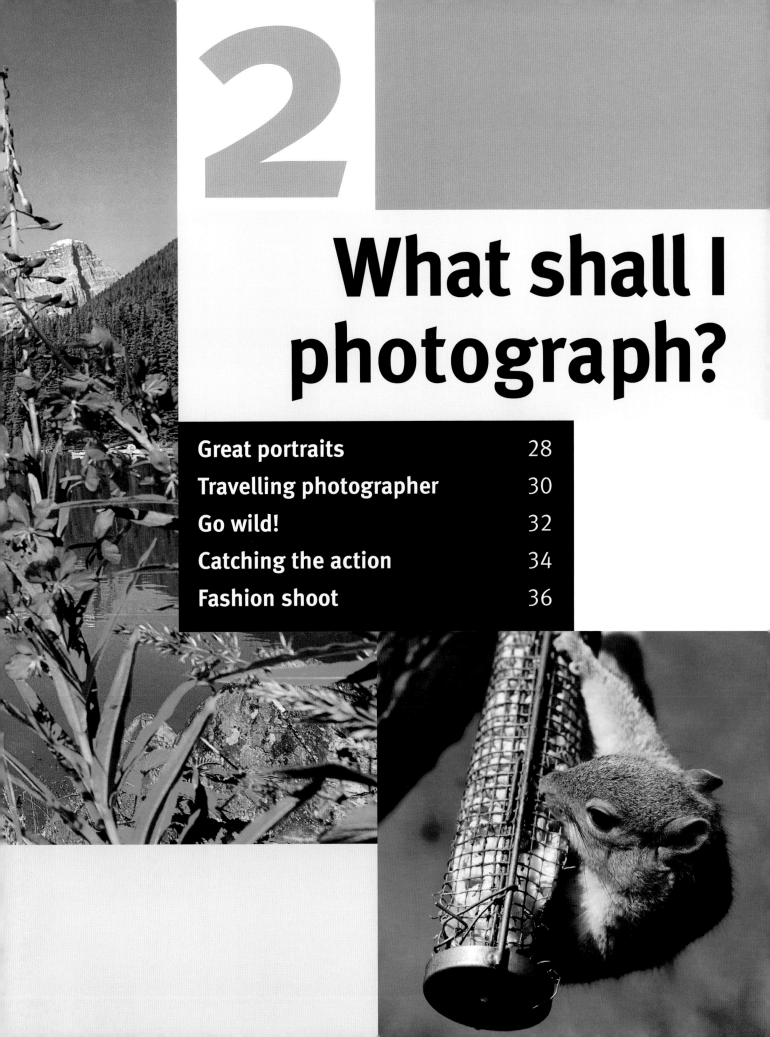

Great portraits

People react unpredictably in front of a camera. Some are quite comfortable, and therefore easy to photograph. Others become tense and awkward, and you'll need to help them relax.

✓ Getting it right

Here are some tips to help you shoot great portraits.

1 Keep shooting The more pictures you take, the more likely you are to get the right shot.

2 Keep talking Explaining what you're doing helps your subject to relax.

3 Use your zoom This is better than getting uncomfortably close.

4 Use playback It helps to show your subject that you're making them look good!

Candid shots are usually natural and informal

Posed pictures can look awkward

✓ Candid or posed?

A posed picture is one that you set up deliberately. You decide where you want to position your subject, what's in the background, and what props to include. Candid shots are much more spontaneous. They may not be as good technically, but they're likely to be full of life.

TECH TIP

Taking self-portraits

If you want to take a picture of yourself – alone or in a group – you will need to use the self-timer function on your camera. First, you should rest the camera on a tripod, table, or other firm surface, then ask everyone else to get into position. Set the time delay, count down aloud while you quickly join the group, then all smile as the shutter fires.

Set the timer on your camera

Use a tripod to keep the camera steady

Capturing personality
A good way of conveying what someone is really like is to photograph them doing one of their favourite activities. This shot zooms in close on the girl's expression of concentration as her hands shape the clay on her potter's wheel.

Character shots
Elderly people often have faces that are full of character. To capture this, zoom in close and ask them to look directly into the camera lens. Later, you might decide to convert a colour shot into black-and-white or sepia on your computer.

Making people look good

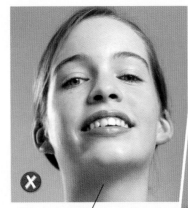

From a low angle we're looking up her nose!

An eye-level, three-quarter view

The best angle
The most flattering photos tend to be shot at your subject's eye level. It often helps if their face is turned at a slight angle, too. The least flattering photos are those shot from below – the emphasis is all on the chin and nostrils, with small eyes, big ears, and no hair.

Telephoto settings are always more flattering

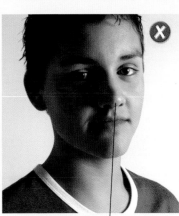

Close-up wide-angle shots can distort chins, noses, and foreheads

Close-up or far away?
It's better to keep your distance and zoom in to fill the frame with your subject's face than it is to move close and zoom out to a wide-angle. Being very close distorts and exaggerates facial features – very unflattering.

Travelling photographer

The best travel photos are almost always ones that are out of the ordinary. They're very rarely the classic tourist views – those have been seen so often that they've become too familiar. Often, the secret lies in getting away from the crowds and finding the shots that no-one else is taking.

A standard tourist shot with no sense of drama or scale

Getting it right
Learn to look for what's interesting, what's unusual, and what captures the atmosphere of a place.

1 **Explore** Get off the beaten track – search for new angles and views.

2 **Include people** Local people really convey the character of a place.

3 **Focus on details** Close-ups are an alternative to the predictable postcard views that we're used to seeing.

4 **Keep a photo journal** Plan ahead for the slideshow you'll make when you get home.

Dynamic angles
Tall buildings are at their most dramatic when photographed from below, looking up at an extreme angle. They are never as impressive when seen flat-on in the middle distance. This worm's-eye view of the Eiffel Tower in Paris was shot in the evening, after the lights had been turned on.

TECH TIP

Photographing sunsets

When set to automatic, most digital cameras will cope with sunsets pretty well. However, because light levels are low and exposures are quite long, you must make sure the camera is held steady. Frame your shot to get some interesting silhouettes in the foreground, and use your zoom to make the sun appear as large as possible. Do not look directly at the sun itself except in your camera's LCD screen.

Photographing landscapes

Landscape photography is always a challenge. In photos, the scenery rarely looks as big or as beautiful as it did when you were actually there. Careful framing that includes something in the foreground and avoids a boring expanse of empty sky will help to give a sense of scale.

Almost half the picture is plain blue sky

Flowers add colour and scale, and lead the eye into the picture

Nothing in the foreground indicates how large or far away the mountains are

An overhead shot gives a different view on things

A bird's-eye view

Shooting from overhead produces unexpected and unusual views that are always interesting. This shot was taken looking down from a bridge as the fruit-seller's boat passed slowly beneath.

Local characters

Street markets are a good place for candid shots of local characters and customs – and amidst the bustle you can stay fairly inconspicuous. Most people won't mind being photographed, but if they're uncomfortable, don't persist.

Go wild!

You don't need exotic, foreign locations for great animal photographs. So don't worry if you can't go on safari, trek through the rainforest, or visit the Antarctic. Instead, take pictures of your pets, or of animals and birds in your backyard. And take your camera with you on a visit to the zoo. All the best wildlife photographers started the same way.

✓ Getting it right

Here are some tips to help you get great wildlife shots.

1 Be patient Get to know the animal's routine, and watch and wait for the perfect moment.

2 Move slowly Don't make sudden noises or movements.

3 Use your zoom Get in as close on your subject as you can.

4 Turn off your flash It may frighten animals away.

5 Turn down the volume If you can, switch off your camera's shutter sound.

Squirrel blends into background

✗ What went wrong?

This squirrel is a long way from the camera so, even with a zoom, it's too small in the picture. And, because it is the same colour as the background, it's even harder to see. The best way to improve this shot is to crop in closer on your computer.

TECH TIP

Getting really close

Some cameras have a special "macro" setting that lets you focus on subjects as close as 5cm (2in) from the lens – ideal for extreme close-up shots of ladybirds, caterpillars, beetles, snails, and other creepy crawlies. A small, inexpensive tripod will keep your camera still and help avoid blurred shots. To ensure that you don't jog the camera when you press the shutter button, use the self-timer.

Use a mini tripod to avoid camera shake

On location

On the farm
Farm animals are usually used to people and unlikely to be spooked by a camera – for an unusual face-to-face shot like this, set your zoom to its widest setting and get as close as you can.

At the zoo
Hopefully the zoo is as close as you'll ever get to dangerous animals – you can shoot through the glass or cage if your camera lens is right up close. Bars or mesh will be so out of focus that they become invisible.

In the garden
Hanging a bird feeder in your garden is an easy way to attract birds and encourage them to pose for your camera – get to know your visitors and let them get used to your presence.

In the park
Most photos of animals are better if you get as near as you can, but deer are notoriously shy. If you approach them slowly and quietly, then keep still and be patient, they may forget you're there.

At home
The best shots of pets are like shots of people – they capture a sense of their personality. Photograph your pet doing what it does best or most often, whether it's eating, playing, or sleeping.

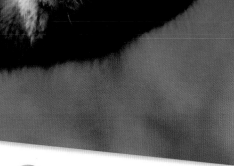

Picture perfect
Here's a great shot of a squirrel showing off its talent for acrobatics. The photographer was able to get close because the animal was intent on eating. This is a strong composition, with the squirrel in the centre of the picture and without a lot of distracting clutter. The squirrel's face is in sharp focus, but the bright blue background is nicely blurred.

Catching the action

At most big sports events you'll see professional photographers with enormous lenses. They need them to get those amazing shots that really give you a sense of the action. Even though your camera may not have a big lens, there's plenty you can do to take some really great sports photos.

✓ Getting it right
Here are some tips to help you shoot exciting sports photos.

1 **Get in position** Work out in advance where you should be.

2 **Anticipate the action** Try to predict what's going to happen so you're ready at the crucial moment.

3 **Use your zoom** Telephoto shots really put you in the thick of the action.

4 **Use fast shutter speeds** Increase your ISO if you can.

5 **Keep shooting** Set your camera to shoot a continuous series of pictures in a single burst.

✗ What went wrong
In some ways, this is not a bad picture: the boy is in focus and frozen in mid-air. But the front-on view doesn't convey much sense of speed, the street scene in the background is cluttered, and of course, there's that awkwardly placed lamppost.

Distracting background

Lamppost cuts through figure

✓ Right place, right moment
When you're photographing a repetitive sequence of moves in which your subject keeps returning to the same position, get in place, pre-focus on the right spot, and wait for him to come round again. If you crouch down low and shoot from beneath, your backdrop will be an uncluttered sky.

TECH TIP

Motion blur

There are times when a blurred picture isn't necessarily a bad thing. Here, the two martial arts students are moving so fast that the camera has been unable to freeze the action completely, but instead of spoiling the picture, the blur conveys a great sense of speed and motion.

✓ Get close to the action

How close can you get? Sadly, there's often a limit. At a soccer match, you'll be on the touchline – you can hardly join the players on the pitch. Use your zoom instead.

1 **Zoom in as far as you can**
But beware of using digital zoom – it may not give you the image quality you'll need if you're going to crop (see p.20).

The dark, shadowed areas can be discarded

2 **Crop in on the image** Transfer the image to your computer and delete any areas of the picture that are empty or unnecessary.

3 **Final image** We're now much closer to the action, and the upright rather than horizontal format is better suited to the picture.

Dramatic moments

A cyclist improvises a cooling shower

Not all good sports photos have to be of the action or the game itself. You might get some great pictures if you turn your back on the main event and instead photograph the reactions of the crowd, particularly if you are able to catch the expressions of spectators just at a key moment of anticipation, triumph, or even defeat. Likewise, look for candid shots of competitors tense with concentration as they are poised to begin a race, exhausted at the end of a game, or euphoric as they are awarded the winner's prize.

The emotions of the spectators run as high as the players'

Fashion shoot

Fashion photography is all about style. Just take a look at the pictures you see on TV, in magazines, or on billboards – as long as they're original and eye-catching, then they're doing the job. So here's the perfect opportunity for you to break all the rules!

Graphic background

Off-centre composition

✓ Getting it right
Here, "mistakes" might be just what you're looking for.

1 **Go for angles** Look for weird viewpoints – overhead or ultra low.

2 **Crop in tight** Zoom in close on details – it's OK if the person's face isn't in the shot.

3 **Out of focus?** Perhaps it just doesn't matter – as long as the effect is good.

4 **Experiment with light** Play around with colours, shadows, and reflections.

The graffiti wall is as much a part of the picture as the girl

✓ On location
When you're shooting outdoors, look for locations that will provide interesting or unusual backgrounds. You're just as likely to come across them in urban city centres as in picturesque landscapes.

Ask your model to dance or spin around – she'll look less self-conscious

✓ Capturing movement
You can use your flash to freeze your model in the middle of a movement. Alternatively, rest your camera on a firm surface and turn your flash off so that a slower shutter speed creates motion blur.

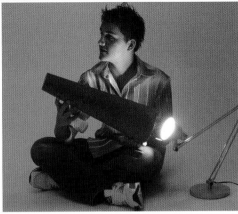

Making a spotlight

A "snoot" turns an ordinary lamp into a spotlight. Roll up some heavy paper or card, and ask a friend to hold it in front of an adjustable lamp. Bulbs can get very hot, so warn your helper not to get too close.

A strong shadow adds atmosphere

✓ Create dramatic shadows

Strong lights placed close to your models can create moody background shadows. Use table or desk lamps and experiment with their positioning until you get the diffused or sharp-edged shadows you want.

Adjustable desk lamps let you position and direct the light exactly where you want it

TECH TIP

Playing with coloured lights

For a fashion shoot, unrealistic colours aren't a problem. In fact, they can create great effects. So, try fitting lamps with different coloured light bulbs and pointing them at your model. You can also cut out homemade "gels" from sheets of coloured cellophane and place them over windows or lights – just like they still do in the theatre and when making movies.

Multiple lights Two different lights were used here – blue from the left and red from the right.

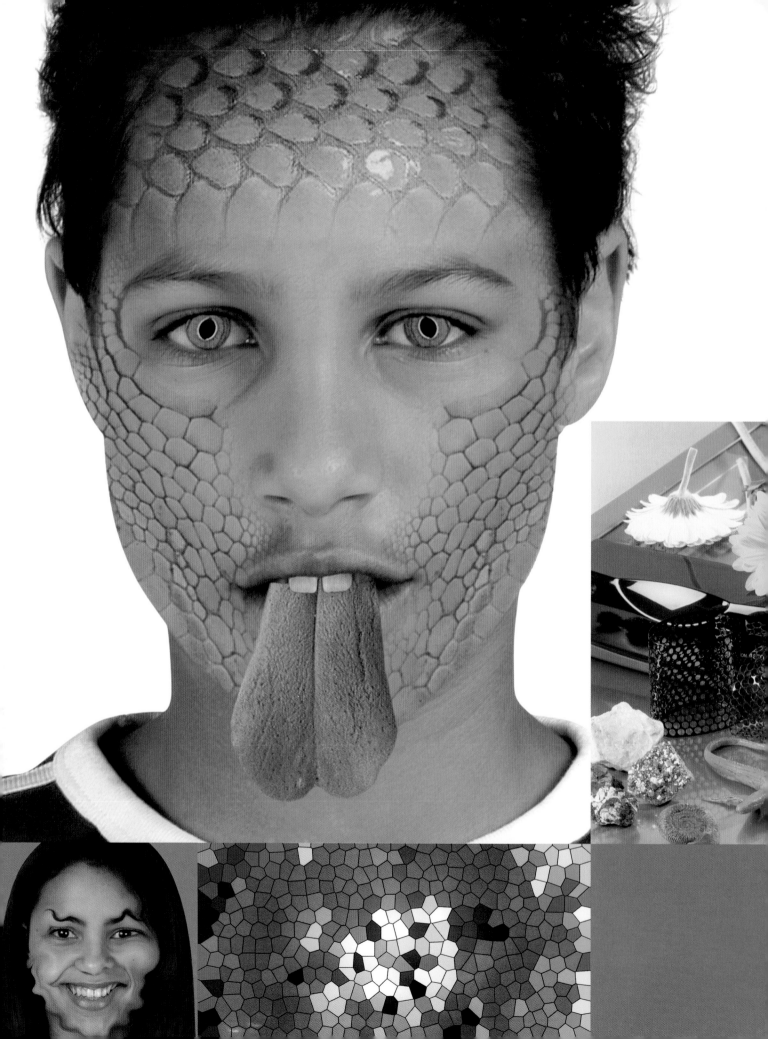

3

Digital trickery

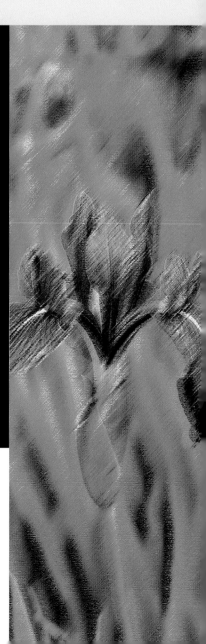

From camera to computer

Your camera stores your photos on a memory card – they will stay here until you delete them. Before you do, though, you should transfer or "download" them to your computer where you can both manipulate them and store them safely.

Camera's memory card slots into card reader

USB connection

Your camera will come with a special cable (known as a USB cable) for connecting it to a computer. The first time you use it, you may have to install some software on your computer. Then you can copy photos from your camera.

Memory card readers

Alternatively, you can remove the memory card from your camera and slot it into a special card reader connected to your computer. Downloading photos this way does not drain the camera battery.

Use thumbnail images to search and sort your photos

TECH TIP

Backing up photos

Backing up may sound boring, but it's really important. Computers can go wrong, hard drives can crash, and it's all too easy to accidentally erase a folder of pictures. Imagine losing all your photos and being unable ever to get them back. So, get into the habit of making back-up copies on a second hard drive or on CDs that you can store in a safe place.

Recordable CDs for archiving

Picture CD inserts for quick reference

Viewing your photos

When you download photos from your camera, they are transferred as digital "image files". Software on your computer will display them on-screen as miniature thumbnails. You can then easily name them, organize them into sets, and enlarge them in order to edit them.

The quick 5-step edit

Here's a way of instantly improving every photo you take. It only takes about two minutes per picture – and almost every time it's worth the effort.

1 Open your photo
Use a simple image-editing application on your computer to view the image.

2 Rotate it If you shot the picture vertically but it's displayed sideways on screen, you'll need to turn it around.

3 Make it straight
This is your chance to straighten up any sloping horizons or buildings that are not quite vertical.

Picture rotated to the left to straighten crooked horizon

4 Crop it You can greatly improve your picture by cropping in to the most interesting bit. Draw a box around the area you want to keep and discard the rest.

Crop to zoom in a little closer

5 The perfect photo! Save the picture as a new image file and give it a name that you'll recognize – perhaps include the date. You might want to store the original, unedited photo as a back-up.

Improving photos

Almost any ordinary photo can be made to look great once you start manipulating it on your computer. Dull shots can be brightened and colours made richer or more natural, and even horrible mistakes can sometimes be fixed. Image-editing software packages vary in what they allow you to do, but all but the most basic will let you make the quick fixes shown here.

✓ Brightness and contrast

Is your picture dull and flat looking? If it is, you'll want to brighten it up and increase the contrast. Usually, this is done with slider controls so that you can see the effect you're having. But you might also find a button called "Enhance" or "Smart Fix" that does the job with one click.

Insufficient contrast means pure whites and blacks are too grey

White snow often picks up a blue or grey colour cast from the sky

✓ Removing colour casts

Photos with an overall tint are said to have a "colour cast". This can be caused by the changes in the colour of natural light at different times of the day or by the colour of artificial indoor lights. Cameras normally compensate for colour cast automatically, but you can easily increase or reduce selected colours on your computer.

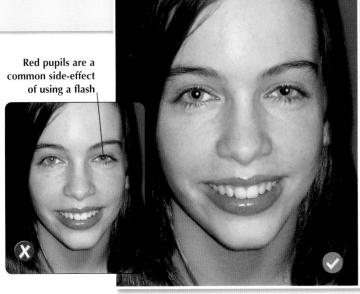

Red pupils are a common side-effect of using a flash

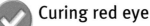

Curing red eye

Firing your flash straight into someone's eyes may give them red pupils. Image-editing applications often have a one-click "Red Eye Removal Tool" that changes the red to black. If not, you may have to select the red area yourself and replace it with black.

Retouching photos

Pictures can be spoilt by unwanted elements – street signs, overhead cables, litter, graffiti, and so on. These can be removed or "retouched" almost as easily as if you were using an eraser on a drawing. You simply copy a small area from one part of your photo and paste it over the area you want to obscure.

A lamppost in the background spoils this shot

A crosshair shows the area being copied

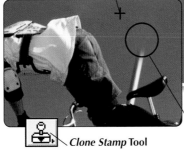

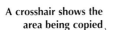
Clone Stamp Tool

A circle indicates the area being erased/replaced

Sharpening increases contrast and makes edges look more clearly defined

Sharpening images

Your photos may look slightly soft or out of focus when downloaded straight from the camera. Sharpening them increases the contrast of edges, strengthens outlines, and makes the picture appear sharper. But beware: don't over-sharpen. If you go too far, your images will begin to look strange. Also, if your original photo is badly out of focus, no amount of sharpening will make it look good.

Create works of art

All image-editing packages have special-effects filters that can turn photos into paintings and sketches. They're usually "one-click" tools – you choose the various settings you want, you check a preview, and then the computer takes a minute or so to process the new picture.

Paper cutouts

The *Cutout* filter creates pictures that look as if they've been made from shapes cut out of coloured paper or even screenprinted. Almost all the details here are reduced to simple outlines and flat colours.

Paint effects

Paint Daubs is one of the many artistic filters that can make a photograph look like a painting. Experiment with different brush settings to make the details look slightly smudged and the colours simplified.

Colours and shapes are simplified to look like brush strokes

All colours in the original photo that are similar in shade are reduced to a single flat area of colour

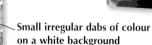

Small irregular dabs of colour on a white background

Pointillist paintings

The French Pointillist painters produced pictures made up of thousands of tiny dabs of paint. The *Pointillize* filter does the same thing. It turns a detailed photo into a patchwork of simple, coloured brushmarks.

Adding texture

We're used to seeing photos on smooth, plain paper, but of course drawings and paintings are often on thick, textured papers or canvas. Here's how to mimic the effect.

❶ Select the *Texturizer* filter Choose a preset texture – in this case *Burlap* (like rough cloth).

❷ Choose how rough or smooth Use the slider controls to determine the "bumpiness" of the surface texture, then decide from which direction you want the light to shine on it.

Preview a close-up of the canvas effect

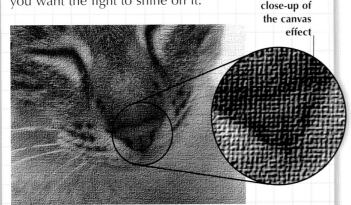

Change the foreground colour to black before applying the filter

Charcoal sketches

Charcoal is one of several sketch filters used to turn photos into drawings. You can vary the thickness of the charcoal lines and the amount of detail in the drawing. You can choose any colour you like for the foreground and background.

Choose a texture to give the surface of the picture a 3D look

Stained glass

This filter puts a grid of irregular polygons or "cells" over your photo, outlined in black like the lead around the pieces of glass in a stained-glass window. Inside each polygon, different tones are reduced to a single flat colour.

Make your coloured cells as big as you like

Pastel effects

The *Rough Pastel* filter combines the effect of pastel crayon strokes with different underlying textures, such as canvas, cloth, or even stone. It creates a soft, hand-drawn look that, done carefully, can look just like the real thing.

Freaky filters

All these special effects are about distortion. They're all filters that let you create weird, swirling, or bloated effects by smearing and stirring around the pixels as if your photo was a painting that hadn't yet dried.

The *Liquify* filter

There are a number of different tools within the *Liquify* filter for you to manipulate your image. *Warp*, *Pucker*, and *Bloat* are the best fun and the most dramatic. Using them is like painting with melting pixels!

Before

Click and drag to create a wavy chin

Add some curls to the eyebrows

Warp Now you can make lines and edges as wavy and curvy as you like. Using the *Warp* tool is a bit like rubbing the tip of your finger across the surface of wet paint. First, you choose a brush setting, then you click and drag your mouse in any direction to smudge or smear your image.

One-click filters

These filters operate on the whole picture rather than just a selected part of it. This makes them very quick and easy to use. If you want to apply a filter to someone's face, it's best to crop your photo first. Choose a square format, and make sure the head is centred.

Twirl

This filter is a bit like spinning a photo on a turntable. The image is twisted and distorted in a circular pattern. The rotation is more extreme in the middle of the image than at the edges.

Bloat The *Bloat* tool works like a magnifying glass. It appears on screen as a circle, which you can vary in size. When you hold down the mouse button, everything beneath the circle becomes enlarged.

Click over one eye to enlarge it

Each time you click, the teeth get bigger

Before

Before

Pucker **and** ***Bloat*** The *Pucker* tool – or *Pinch*, as it's sometimes called – squeezes everything you click on, so that it gets compressed into a smaller space. Puckering this girl's fingers and bloating the tips gives her hands like a frog's feet.

Bloat tool for sucker-like fingertips

Pinch and drag downwards for a pointed chin

Pinch

The *Pinch* filter squeezes the central part of a picture into a small space in the middle and makes the outside edges long and stretched – it's great for creating enormous hair, long chins, and sticking-out ears.

Spherize

This filter wraps a photograph around the surface of a ball, a bit like the skin on an orange. If you want to create really exaggerated effects, apply the filter several times in a row.

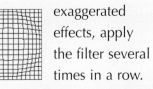

Go crazy with colour

Here's where you can have fun playing around. Once your pictures are on your computer, you can exaggerate colours, swap them for different ones, create psychedelic special effects, or produce stylish black-and-white shots.

Greens swap with pinks when you invert colours

Colours become simpler and more intense as you increase the contrast

Swapping colours around

Using *Invert* is a quick and easy way of producing crazy colour effects. With black-and-white images it turns black to white and white to black. With colour images, it swaps each colour for its opposite.

Ramping up the colour

Increasing the contrast has a weird effect on colours. Any subtle shades in the original photo disappear and are replaced by areas of pure white, pure black, and super-saturated colour.

TECH TIP

What's your favourite colour?

Pick the colour you want to replace

Don't much like yellow cars? Always dreamed of a red Ferrari? Nothing could be easier. Most image-editing applications allow you to replace one colour with another. Use the eyedropper tool to click on and select the areas of the picture that are the colour you want to change. Then use *Hue/Saturation* sliders to create a sample of the colour you want. Now just click OK.

Replace colour

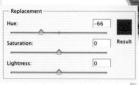

Yellow turns magically to red

Old-style pictures

Some digital cameras will shoot in black-and-white or sepia. But you'll get better quality if you shoot in colour and tweak the picture later.

Artistic black-and-white

Always make a copy of your original photo before you turn it into black-and-white. Once you've discarded the colour, you can't get it back.

1 Choose a graphic image Look for bold shapes and strong outlines.

2 Convert to black-and-white Use the *Greyscale*, *Replace Colour*, or *Colourize* command in the image-editing software on your computer.

Increase the contrast for darker blacks and brighter whites

A rosy pink light has been created by slightly altering the overall hue

Colour makeover

Two things have been done to transform this picture. First, the entire photo has been given a pink colour cast, done by using the sliders in the *Hue/Saturation* tool. Second, the turquoise shutters and the blue of the old man's shirt have been turned purple, done with the *Replace Colour* command (see left).

Nostalgic sepia

Sepia photographs have a historical feel, so it's an effect that works best with family portraits or landscapes, rather than modern-day street scenes.

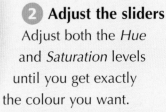

1 Open *Hue/Saturation* Click on *Colourize* to convert your picture to a single colour.

2 Adjust the sliders Adjust both the *Hue* and *Saturation* levels until you get exactly the colour you want.

Create an oval-shaped vignette

Photo magic

Once your digital photos are on your computer, you can start to have fun with them. Cut out an element from one shot and paste it into another one, remove a background and replace it with something different, swap your friends' heads around, or make spooky ghost montages. Just let your imagination run free.

Original images

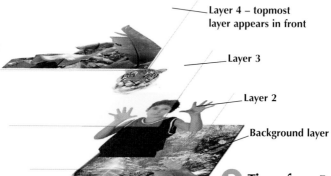

Layer 4 – topmost layer appears in front

Layer 3

Layer 2

Background layer

1 Original photos This montage starts with three pictures. The boy is outlined using a "selection" tool so that his background can be cut away. The tiger's head is separated from its body.

2 The four-layer sandwich A fourth image is created by duplicating just the foreground leaves at the front of the jungle picture. The tiger and boy are re-sized to match, then all four images are overlaid on top of one another in separate layers.

3 Tiger face Each layer is opaque, so the boy appears behind the foreground leaves and in front of the jungle background. The tiger's head obscures the boy's face beneath – a little blurring under the chin disguises the join.

TECH TIP

How to cut out a background

In order to isolate part of a digital photo – so that you can cut it out, alter it, or copy it – you have to "select" it. There are several tools for making selections.

1 Selecting The lasso tool lets you use your mouse to draw an outline around the edge of what you want to select. A line of moving dashes called "marching ants" shows the area you've selected.

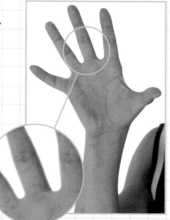

2 Deleting Once you've created a path around the area you want to cut out, you can delete the background.

3 Softening edges Feathering is a way of softening hard edges. It blurs pixels at the edge of a selection and helps hide any visible joins.

Creating ghosts

If the layers in a montage picture are made semi-transparent, they become see-through. When this technique is applied to a photograph of a person, the effect is spookily ghost-like.

❶ Gathering images
Start by assembling the different pictures you need. Either shoot them specially or use a scanner to digitize them (see page 56).

Look for images in magazines or books

❷ Cutouts and layers
Make a selection around the outline of your figure and delete its background. Put it on a separate layer.

Soften the edges by feathering or by using a filter such as *Diffuse Glow*

Adjust the opacity to make the layer slightly see-through

Don't forget you can re-size and flip (reverse) the figure to fit the background

❸ Haunted house To make your ghost convincing, give her a spooky, other-worldly look by turning her almost black-and-white, and make her semi-transparent so that she appears to float over the background.

The secrets of layers

Digital-photo special effects are usually created on the computer by sandwiching or layering different images on top of one another.

Opaque layers When the layer on top is made opaque, it hides or masks what's underneath it.

Semi-transparent layers The top layer can be made semi-transparent so that the image on the layer beneath can be seen through it – creating a blending effect.

Complex images Montage pictures can have dozens of opaque or semi-transparent layers. They can be switched on or off while you work so you can see the effects they create when they're combined.

Fantasy makeovers

The more skilful you get at using imaging software on the computer, the more creative you can be, and the more fun you can have playing around with ordinary photos. See what you'd look like with a different hair or eye colour, or have fun turning your friends into mutants.

Crazy make-up

Make all the changes shown here on separate layers. This means you can turn them on and off, or change your mind and start again if you need to.

Elliptical Marquee tool

Make a selection of each iris to restrict the colour change to the eyes. Spray on green eye shadow with an airbrush

Lasso tool

1 **Change eye colour** Make the girl's eyes bright turquoise blue by duplicating the background layer, selecting the eyes, and using the eyedropper in *Replace Colour*.

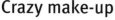

To make the effect appear natural, turn the newly coloured layer semi-transparent

2 **Change hair colour** Copy the background layer and make a freehand selection of the girl's hair. Use the *Hue/Saturation* tool to change the colour, and set the layer to semi-transparent.

Magic Wand tool

3 **Whitening teeth** On a copy layer, select just the teeth. Change them to pure white, but make the upper layer semi-transparent to avoid an unnatural look.

Lighten the teeth with *Hue/Saturation* then set the opacity to about 30%. Use the same tool to apply digital lipstick in any colour you like

4 **Remove blemishes** Spots, scars, and skin rashes can be magically erased using the *Healing Brush*. It uses samples of perfect skin to conceal blemishes.

Making monsters

Adding reptile eyes and a lolling dog's tongue to a portrait shot is pretty straightforward. Changing the colour and texture of skin presents slightly more of a challenge.

1 **Adding an alien skin** Make small selections of areas of snake and lizard skin, and drag them into new layers on top of your original photo. Rotate and re-size the samples, and position them over the boy's forehead and cheeks. Adjust the opacity to make them semi-transparent. Use the *Hue/Saturation* tool to change the colour.

2 **Adding the lizard's eye** Find an image of a suitable eye. Carefully select it and delete the background. Drag it into a new layer above the existing ones. Resize it and position it over the boy's eye.

3 **Adding the dog's tongue** Cut out the tongue and lengthen it using a *Liquify* filter. Paste it into a new layer and make it fit with the boy's teeth.

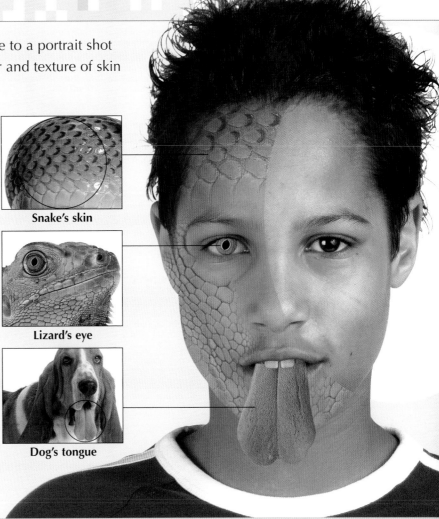

Snake's skin

Lizard's eye

Dog's tongue

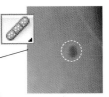

Click on an area of unblemished skin with the *Healing Brush*, then on a spot. Watch it disappear!

TECH TIP

Layer opacity

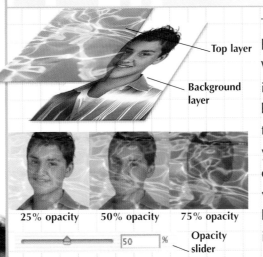

Top layer

Background layer

25% opacity   50% opacity   75% opacity

50 %   Opacity slider

The opacity of a layer describes how easily you can see through it. When it's opaque (100 per cent), it completely obscures the layer beneath it. When it's entirely see-through (0 per cent), it's as though you're looking through a clear piece of glass to the layer below. At any value in between, the layer will be semi-transparent and the two images will blend into each other.

Panoramas

Joining together a series of separate photographs to create a panorama is a process called "photomerging" or "photostitching", and it's something that most image-editing programs will help you to do automatically. However, successful results depend on having the right set of photos in the first place.

Creating a photomerge

Here's a picture that would have been difficult to create in any other way. The girl appears in three different places at once. Of course, these are three separate pictures that have been merged.

1 Take a series of photos Stand still, shoot portrait shots rather than landscape shots, keep the zoom lens setting the same, and keep the horizon level.

2 Combine your images Open your photomerge software, select the pictures you want to stitch together, click OK, and watch as the program automatically matches up your shots and drops them into position, neatly overlapping one another.

Original three images

3 Crop the final image Delete any unwanted areas from the top and bottom, and retouch any obvious joins.

Overlap your pictures by about 30 per cent – they're easier to combine

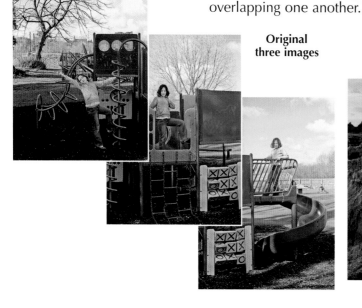

TECH TIP

Blending panoramic shots

Sometimes photostitching software finds it hard to make invisible, seamless joins. Where shots overlap, you may see telltale bands or streaks of colour – particularly in areas of sky. To solve this, you'll need to do a bit of retouching after the photomerge has been completed. Use the *Clone Stamp* tool to sample small areas of colour from either side of the join, and paste them over the top. Work slowly and carefully, on just one small area at a time.

Clone Stamp tool

Sky before blending shows visible join

Sky after blending

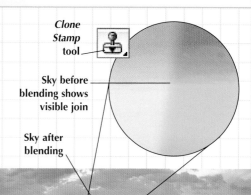

Using a scanner

A scanner is actually just a big digital camera. It takes a digital photograph of whatever you place on its glass. The difference between it and a regular camera is that its image sensor moves back and forth, progressively scanning the object to capture a digital image of it.

Old photos and artworks

Scanning old family photographs is a perfect way of preserving and restoring them. Once they're on the computer, you can mend tears, clean up scratches, and restore faded colours. The same goes for drawings, paintings, and other pictures.

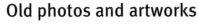

TECH TIP

Good and bad scans

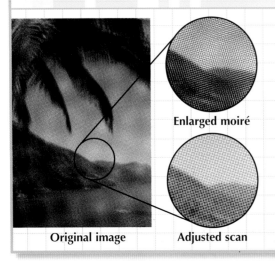

Enlarged moiré

Original image

Adjusted scan

Images from magazines or books can pick up odd patterns when scanned. Called "moiré patterns", they are caused by the pattern of ink dots in the original clashing with the pattern of pixels. To avoid them, angle the original picture slightly differently and re-scan.

Using your scanner as a camera

Don't stop at scanning photographic prints and other flat pieces of paper. You can scan anything that will fit safely on the scanner's glass, such as flowers, stones, shells, leaves, toys, jewellery, buttons, coins, and stamps. You can even scan your own hands (you need to keep them very still). However, bear in mind that only what's actually touching the glass will be in sharp focus.

Scanner trickery

It is easy to create combined digital images or "photomontages" with the help of a scanner – just collect all the pictures and real-world objects you need and arrange them on the glass.

Original scanned photo of stars

You're on a separate underlying layer

My heroes – and me

Scan a picture of your favourite movie stars and cut them out from their background. Extend the picture area so that there is space to add a cutout photo of you on the end of the row.

Fresh or dried flower heads and leaves

Scanned borders and frames

Arrange a selection of small objects such as flowers, leaves, buttons, or beads on the scanner glass in a frame shape. Once scanned, select and delete the inside of the frame ready for a photo to be added.

Favourite print

Bead border

1 Protecting the scanner glass To avoid scratching the glass, and to keep it clean, place a sheet of transparent acetate over it. Place the objects you wish to scan on top of the acetate.

2 Covering with a cloth If you can't close the lid of the scanner, carefully drape a thick, dark fabric, such as black velvet, over the top. This will prevent an uneven grey or coloured background.

4

It's showtime!

Perfect printing

Many home printers now produce great-looking prints – without the need for a computer. You can either connect your camera to the printer by cable or insert your memory card into a special slot, then print direct. Printers are often surprisingly cheap, too; it's the paper and ink that cost the money.

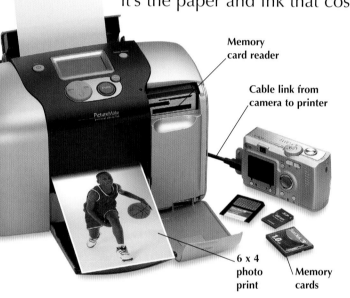

Memory card reader

Cable link from camera to printer

6 x 4 photo print

Memory cards

Compact dedicated photo printer

A4 glossy paper

A4 inkjet printer

Types of printer

By far the most common type is the inkjet, which prints images by squirting droplets of coloured ink through tiny nozzles. The most basic models employ just two ink cartridges – a black one and a colour one. Special photo printers may use up to eight different inks, including two different blacks and even a gloss coating to produce high-quality prints with subtle gradations of colour and tone.

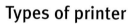

Making giant prints

The best way to make posters or prints larger than your printer can handle, is to print your picture in sections or tiles and then stick them together.

❶ Enlarge the whole image Crop it four times and save each quarter as a new file. Make sure you overlap the sections.

❷ Print out the four tiles Trim them neatly with scissors or a craft knife, line them up accurately, then join them together with invisible tape.

Types of paper

The best paper is thick, glossy, and specially designed for photographs, but it is the most expensive. In fact, you can print on almost anything – from everyday office paper to envelopes, sticky labels, iron-on transfer paper, temporary tattoo paper, and even metallized fridge-magnet paper.

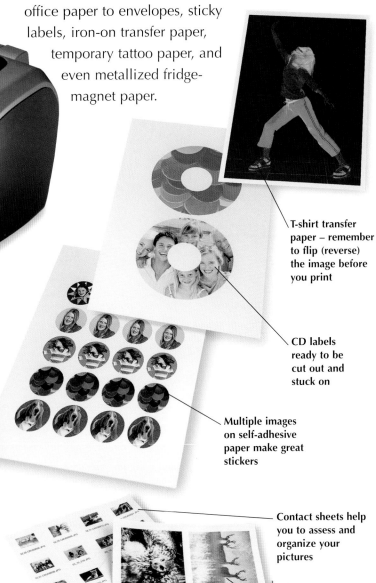

T-shirt transfer paper – remember to flip (reverse) the image before you print

CD labels ready to be cut out and stuck on

Multiple images on self-adhesive paper make great stickers

Contact sheets help you to assess and organize your pictures

Printing four images on a single sheet saves paper

Contact sheets and picture layouts

Don't restrict yourself to one picture per page. Most imaging software lets you print contact sheets; they show thumbnails for a folder full of different images. You can also collate pictures so they resize and print, two, three, or more on a sheet.

Printing problems

Printing trouble is often the result of images being set to the wrong resolution. Remember: the term resolution means the number of pixels from which your photo is made up.

Why is my print so small?

If your photo prints out as a small image in the middle of your sheet of paper, the resolution may be set too high. The pixels are being squeezed closely together – so although the picture quality is good, the size of the print is too small.

Solution: either check the box in the *Print Preview* window that says something like "Scale to fit media" or open the *Image Size* window and reduce the resolution. For most inkjet printers 150 pixels per inch is fine – but you can go even lower.

Why is my print so blocky?

If your photo looks as if it's made up of lots of small square blocks, the resolution is too low. There are simply not enough pixels to print it at the size you're trying for. It will have to be smaller.

Cropping a high-resolution image can mean it prints very small

Solution: either uncheck the "Scale to fit media" box in the *Print Preview* window or open the *Image Size* window and then reduce the height and width of the image.

Low-resolution images printed too large reveal blocky pixels

Creating frames

The right frame can transform a photograph, making an average picture look better and a good one look great. If you can't find just the frame you want, why not create your own on computer before you print out your photo?

Creating your own frame
Choose a photograph, make a duplicate of it, and then create your frame on this copy.

1 Draw a frame Enlarge the size of the canvas to make a frame and then select the photo in the centre and delete it.

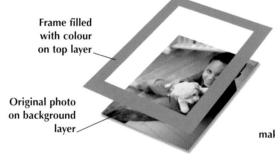

Frame filled with colour on top layer

Original photo on background layer

A simple emboss style makes the frame appear 3D

One-click frames
Pre-set frames often come built-in to image-editing applications. Look in the *Effects* or *Styles* menu for a preview of what's available. Choose one and the software will create the frame around your photo for you automatically.

2 Make the frame a solid colour
Select the frame (instead of the now-transparent hole in the centre) and use the *Fill* tool to add colour or pattern.

3 Create a 3D look
Apply a *Layer Style* to the frame. There are several to choose from. Experiment with different bevel, emboss, and drop-shadow effects.

Adding textures and pattrens
This amazing lizard-skin frame was made by "sampling" the skin of the animal that appears in the photo. Small areas were selected and copied, rotated and re-sized, and then pasted alongside one another to build up the frame, like a patchwork. The spiky edge comes from copying a section of spines from the lizard's back and tail.

Creating metallic surfaces

A combination of special image effects can make a frame look as if it's made of metal.

1 Highlight the layer containing your picture frame, select it, and fill it with an appropriate colour.

2 Duplicate that layer and apply a *Layer Style* such as chrome to it. This adds 3D highlights and shadows. Adjust the opacity of the top layer to see the colour through the metal effect.

Weird and wacky shapes

Do square or rectangular frames seem boring? If so, try cutting out a circular- or oval-shaped frame from a square original, or using the *Eraser* tool to create irregular, ragged edges in any design you like.

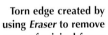

Torn edge created by using *Eraser* to remove areas of original frame

Oval zebra fur frame

A *Layer Style* adds shadows and highlights

Rough, torn frame to suit the peeling paint in the image

Creating vignettes

A vignette is an oval or circular mask with a softly blurred or "feathered" edge. It is often used for portrait shots.

1 **Make a selection** Use the *Elliptical Marquee* tool to draw an oval or a circle. Once you've drawn it, you can drag it with your mouse until it's in the right position.

A low feather value gives a harder edge

2 **Feather the selection** Use a feather value of around 15–20 pixels to create a nicely blurred edge. Now invert the selection and delete the background.

A canvas texture gives a hand-painted look

3 **Add a texture** While the background is still selected, you can create an additional effect. Open the *Texturizer* filter and apply a *Canvas* texture. Then draw another ellipse with the *Marquee* tool and cut out an oval image.

Print shop

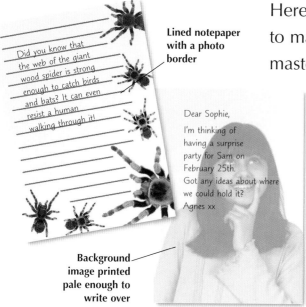

Lined notepaper with a photo border

Did you know that the web of the giant wood spider is strong enough to catch birds and bats? It can even resist a human walking through it!

Dear Sophie,
I'm thinking of having a surprise party for Sam on February 25th. Got any ideas about where we could hold it?
Agnes xx

Background image printed pale enough to write over

Here are some ideas for using your own photographs to make notepaper and greetings cards. But once you've mastered these techniques, don't stop. Why not go on to make party invitations, envelopes, gift tags, and bookmarks – even newsletters and posters?

Personalized stationery

Blank notepaper is best printed on regular inkjet or matte paper, rather than on glossy photo paper. You can add lines to help you keep your handwriting straight or set the opacity of an image to, say, 30 per cent so that it prints as a pale background.

Single-sided greetings cards

This card is printed on a single sheet of paper. It is then folded twice to make a card with a picture on the front as well as one inside.

1 Create a template Divide the page into four equal areas. Size one of your images to fit into one of the quarters, then invert it, and drop it into place. Size four more images to fit together in the front panel.

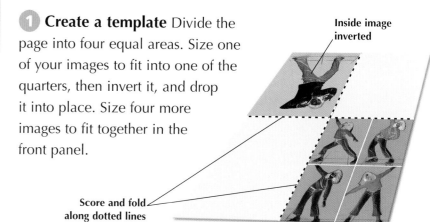

Inside image inverted

Score and fold along dotted lines

Adding words to pictures

Text and pictures can be combined in most word-processing and image-editing software. Here's how to make a postcard from a photo of the Statue of Liberty.

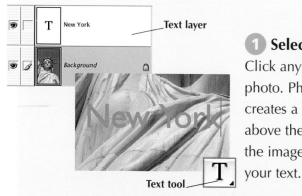

Text layer

Text tool

1 Select the *Type* tool Click anywhere on your photo. Photoshop *Elements* creates a new *Type* layer above the layer containing the image. Now type in your text.

2 Format your text Highlight your text and then choose the font, font size, and font style that you want. Move the text into position by clicking and dragging.

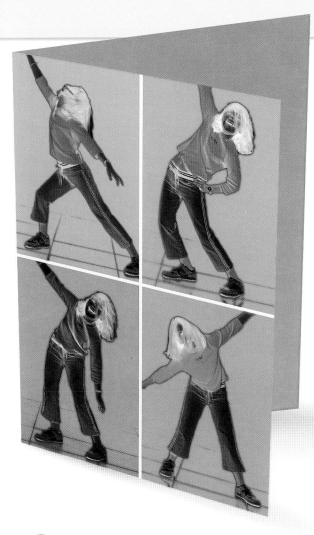

Double-sided cards

This card is made by printing an image on one side of a sheet of paper, then feeding it back through the printer to print on the other side as well.

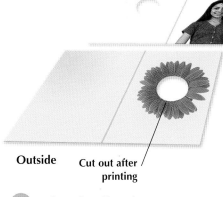

Inside

Outside   Cut out after printing

1 Print the first image
The flowerhead and coloured background will appear on one side of the paper. Open a second image and print it on the other side of the sheet.

2 Cut out a window
Make a circular hole in the centre of the flower and fold the paper so that the image inside peeps through.

2 Score and fold Copy the example opposite. The four small images will appear on the front, and the large image will be inside, the correct way up.

3 Shape the type Use the *Warp Text* tool to do this. Effects vary from the arc shown here to waves, spheres, bulges, and twists. Select the degree of distortion you want.

4 Add a drop shadow
This will lift the letters slightly above the surface of the image. Open the *Layer Styles* menu and choose one of the preset drop shadows.

A white border completes the classic postcard look

Comics and jokes

Have you always wanted to be a cartoonist? But you just can't draw as well as the professionals? Perhaps the answer is to use your own photos instead of drawings. It's easy to add captions and speech bubbles, so you'll be creating your own jokes and comic strips in no time.

Making comic characters

You can add hand-drawn beards, moustaches, glasses, and false noses in most image-editing programs. Create a new empty layer and use the *Brush* tool. Don't draw directly on your original photo.

Draw knock-out stars, speed lines, and other classic cartoon effects

Phony posters

All you need to create a convincing WANTED! poster are a black-and-white mug shot, a sepia-tinted background with tattered edges, and an old-fashioned Wild West font.

Creating a photostory

A photostory is like a cartoon strip made up of photographs. The first thing to do is to create a page or "canvas" large enough for all the pictures you want to include.

1 **Prepare the photos** Exaggerate the colours with the *Hue/Saturation* tool and draw an outline around the figures. Place them in a strip.

2 **Add text blocks** Use preset shapes or drawing shapes using a *Polygonal Lasso* tool. Fill each with a solid colour and give it a black ("stroke") outline.

3 **Write your story** Type in your text and select the right font and size. Drag the text into position, and cut or add words if you need to.

Making speech bubbles

The convention for a speech bubble is an oval shape with a tapered arrow indicating who's speaking. Always add speech bubbles on a new layer, above your original photo.

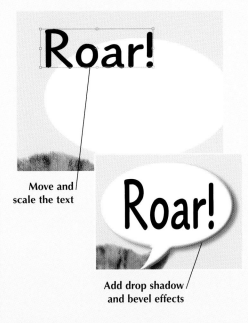

Move and scale the text

Add drop shadow and bevel effects

❶ Draw the speech bubble
Set the foreground colour to white, select the *Custom Shape* tool and a *Talk Bubble* shape, then drag it roughly into position.

❷ Type in your text Adjust the font size and move the text into place. Select the *Shape* layer and add a *Layer Style* drop shadow and bevel to the bubble.

❸ Link the text and shape layers
This means that any changes you make will affect them both. Select the *Move* tool, and click and drag to get the size and position of the bubble just right.

Show the world

A title screen introduces the show

Once you've got a selection of photos you're pleased with, you'll want to show them off. And, because they're digital, there's a lot you can do with them. Make slideshows, burn CDs and DVDs, wear your pictures as tattoos or on your clothes, and share them with friends via the Internet.

Images will be flipped left to right

Slideshows

The key to creating an interesting or entertaining slideshow is to get your pictures to tell a story – whether it's about a person, an event, or a family holiday. So, spend some time putting your shots in the best possible running order.

Temporary tattoos

These tattoos are really transfers (also known as decals). You can create them by printing your photos on to a sheet of special water-slide temporary tattoo paper. Then apply them by pressing the print against your skin, wetting the back, and peeling away the paper layer.

TECH TIP

Slideshow transitions

Most programs used for creating slideshows let you choose the way one picture moves into the next. For example, you can make images dissolve, fade, or wipe.

❶ **Create a folder** Place your slideshow photos in the folder. Number or name them so they are in the right running order.

❷ **Choose a transition effect** Set the length of time you want each photo to be on-screen before it changes to the next.

A *dissolve* slowly swaps pictures pixel by pixel

Email and Internet

The Internet and digital photography were made for each other. You can be your own publisher and share your pictures with anyone, anywhere.

Emailing your photos

Images can be emailed as "file attachments". Before you send an image, make it into a low-resolution email version: shrink the height and width, drop the number of pixels per inch (ppi) to 72ppi, and use JPEG compression to reduce the file size.

Opaque paper stops the colour of the shirt showing through

Web page templates show thumbnails for navigation as well as larger images

Wear your photos!

Is there a better way than this of showing off your pictures? Printed t-shirts can be made using special fabric transfer paper – choose transparent paper for white shirts or opaque paper for coloured shirts. Once you've made your print, you simply cut it out and iron it on.

Creating a web page

Lots of software programs offer templates for making your own web pages. You choose a style you want, sort your photos into a folder, add titles and captions, and the software automatically builds the pages for you. They're then ready to be uploaded to your Internet Service Provider's computer.

Internet safety warning

Always check with your parents before putting anything on the Internet. Do not give out your full name, email address, or telephone number, or reveal the address of where you live.

*A **horizontal blind** uses broad stripes or slats*

Glossary

Aperture The hole that controls how much light passes through a lens. It can be widened to let in more light and narrowed to admit less, so that the photo is correctly exposed. Aperture is measured in f numbers or f stops.

Autofocus The mechanism used by cameras to focus automatically, often on what is in the middle of the frame.

CCD Charge Coupled Device: the array of sensors in a camera or scanner that records a digital image.

Compression Reducing the size of image files using software that either stores data very efficiently or discards details that you may not be able to see. JPEG files use compression.

Contrast The difference in brightness between the light and dark areas of a photograph.

Crop To delete unwanted areas of a photo – from the top, bottom, or sides.

Depth of field The distance between the nearest and farthest points from the camera within which things are in sharp focus.

Digitize To create an image by converting colour and brightness into numbers a computer can understand.

Download To transfer digital images from a camera to a computer or printer.

dpi Dots per inch. A measure of the number of dots that make up a printed picture. The more there are the higher the resolution.

Exposure meter The mechanism used by cameras to measure the amount of light and calculate the right exposure for a photograph.

Feather To soften or blur the boundary between two areas of an image – often used to disguise joins.

File format The form in which a digital image is stored and handled. JPEG is the most common in digital photography.

Filter In image-editing software, filters are used to manipulate or add special effects to photos.

Focus In-focus images are clear and sharply defined; out-of-focus images are soft or blurred.

Focus lock Pressing the shutter halfway down and holding it there lets you focus on a particular subject then re-frame your picture.

Gigabyte (GB) A thousand megabytes.

Greyscale An image made up of black, white, and various shades or tones of grey.

ISO The sensitivity setting of the CCD sensor in a digital camera. The higher the ISO the more sensitive it is, and the better it will be able to take photos in low-light situations.

JPEG The image file format most frequently used for digital photographs.

Layer In image-editing software, layers contain different components of a composite image. They appear in a stack, with the topmost layer showing in the foreground of the picture and the layer at the bottom forming the background.

LCD Liquid Crystal Display. The screen on the back of a digital camera that displays a preview of the picture you are about to take or plays back images you have already recorded.

Lens A series of glass discs or elements through which light enters the camera and is then focused on the CCD image sensor.

Macro Extreme close-up photography.

Megabyte (MB) One million bytes – a measurement of file size. The higher the resolution of an image file the more megabytes it will comprise.

Megapixel One million pixels – a measurement of how many pixels a digital camera uses to record a single photograph.

Memory card The removable card on which digital cameras store photos. Their capacity is measured in megabytes or gigabytes.

Opacity The degree to which an image layer is see-through, semi-transparent, or opaque.

Pixel Short for "picture element", a pixel is a tiny single unit of colour and brightness in a digital image. It is a single square of light on a computer monitor.

ppi Pixels per inch. A measure of the number of pixels that make up a digital image. The more there are the higher the resolution.

Red eye An effect where flash makes the pupils of someone's eyes appear red instead of black.

Resolution The degree of detail in a digital image – measured in ppi.

Scanner A device for creating digitized image files from print, film, or even 3D originals.

Self-timer A camera mechanism that allows a time delay between pressing the shutter and the photo being taken.

Shutter Mechanism that opens for a controlled length of time to allow light to fall on the camera's CCD image sensor.

Telephoto The zoom lens setting that magnifies distant subjects – like a telescope.

USB A type of cable that is used to connect cameras, computers, scanners, and printers.

White balance The camera's automatic compensation for light that has a colour cast – indoors, at dawn, at sunset, etc.

Wide angle The zoom lens setting that captures the broadest angle-of-view of a scene.

Zoom A camera lens that can be varied between telephoto and wide-angle.

Index

Online resources

There is a lot of information about digital photography on the web. The best sites are those created by software publishers and hardware manufacturers – in particular Adobe, the creator of Photoshop. They offer practical advice, projects, activities, and photo galleries.

Adobe Digital Kids Club
www.adobe.com/education/digkids
Lots of information about digital photography (and video, too). Tips on how to take better pictures, free online tutorials on how to use Adobe software packages, and photo galleries to which you can submit your own photos.

Agfa Digital Photo Course
www.agfanet.com/en/cafe/ photocourse/digicourse
A 20-part teaching course all about digital photography.

Kodak Online Guide to Taking Great Pictures
www.kodak.com/eknec/PageQuerier. jhtml?pq-path=38&pq-locale=en_US
Articles and advice not just on taking pictures but also on editing, printing, and sharing them – with a regularly changing Picture of the Day.

HP Digital Photography Centre
h30015.www3.hp.com/ hp_dpc/home/home.asp
Hewlett Packard site containing advice and information on digital photography. Linked to an Activity Centre with lots of ideas for practical projects.

Microsoft Digital Photography
www.microsoft.com/windowsxp/using/di gitalphotography/default.mspx
A site about using digital photographs with Windows XP – includes how-to advice on cameras, as well as on taking and editing pictures.

Apple iPhoto
www.apple.com/ilife/iphoto
Apple site about iPhoto, the image editing and cataloguing application built into OS X.

ShortCourses
www.shortcourses.com
A selection of complete books online covering how digital cameras work.

Digital Photography Review
www.dpreview.com
A site for grown-ups, but one of the best for detailed reviews of new digital cameras. Includes a good illustrated glossary of technical words.

The SimCam
www.photonhead.com/simcam
An interactive virtual camera you can use online to take pictures and learn about shutter speeds, aperture, zoom lenses, and camera shake.

Acknowledgements

Models **Ella Ainsworth, Max Buckingham, Charlotte Cooper, Kwade Davis, Ben Grice, Joanna Harris, Barney King, Lydia, Alice Nicholson, Christina Pepper, Chenoa Pugh, Naadirah Qazi, Beth Rylance, Rebecca Tasker, Trooper the dog**

Photography **Andy Crawford, Dave King**

Index **Hilary Bird**

The publisher would like to thank the following for their kind permission to reproduce their photographs:
t = top, b = bottom, l = left,
r = right, c = centre, a = above

3 Getty Images: James Muldowney (br). **4 Alan Buckingham:** (bl), (cr); **Getty Images:** Georgette Douwma (br). **4-5 Alan Buckingham:** (t). **5 Getty Images:** (bl). **6 Alan Buckingham:** (bl). **7 Corbis Royalty Free Images:** (b). **9 Courtesy of apple mac computers:** (br); **Courtesy of Olympus:** (cr). **10 Image Courtesy of Lexar Media:** (bcl), (bcr); **Sandisk ® Corporation:** (bc). **14 Alan Buckingham:** (bc), (clb); **Andy Pepper:** (c). **15 Alan Buckingham:** (bl), (br), (cla), (tl), (tr), (c). **16 Corbis:** Tom Stuart (ca), (tr). **18 Alan Buckingham:** (br), (cl), (tr). **19 Corbis:** Steve Terrill (tc); **Corbis Royalty Free Images:** (cb); **Getty Images:** Antonio Mo (tr); Beateworks/Dana Hoff (bl); Charles Krebs (cl). **20 Corbis Royalty Free Images:** (bl); **Chris George:** (c), (cl). **20-21 Chris George:** (t). **22 Alan Buckingham:** (tr); **Chris George:** (cl). **24 Chris George:** (ca), (tr). **25 Andy Pepper:** (c), (cla), (cra), (tr). **26 John Beardsworth:** (bl); **Empics Ltd:** Phil Noble (bc). **26-27 Eyewire. 27 Getty Images:** Georgette Douwma (br). **28 Getty Images:** Greg Ceo (c); James Muldowney (tr); **Zefa Visual Media:** R. Lewine (bl). **29 Corbis:** Tom Stewart (tl); **Getty Images:** Tom Morrison (cl). **30 John Beardsworth:** (l). **31 Corbis:** Mike McQueen (cr); Nevada Wier (bl); **Eyewire:** (ca), (tr). **32 Corbis:** Robert Pickett c; Wolfgang Kaehler (bl). **32-33 Getty Images:** Georgette Douwma. **33 Corbis:** Don Mason (bc); Eric and David Hosking c; Joe McDonald (cra); Tom Brakefield (crb); **Corbis Royalty Free Images:** (tc). **34 Alamy Images:** Richard Greenhill (b); **Corbis:** David Stoecklein (bl); **Getty Images:** Joe McBride (cr). **35 Corbis:** Mark Gamba (tl); **Empics Ltd:** Phil Noble (br). **36 Zefa Visual Media:** astra productions (ca); Masterfile/Dennie Cody (tr). **38 Alan Buckingham:** (bc). **40 Science & Society Picture Library:** (bl). **41 Zefa/Stockdisc:** (x5). **42 Getty Images:** Frans Lemmens (bl), (cr). **43 Alamy Images:** Shotfile (cl), (cr); **Chris George:** (bl). **44 Alan Buckingham:** (cla), (crb); **Chris George:** (bl). **45 Alan Buckingham:** (bl). **48 Alan Buckingham:** (cra). **49 Louise Thomas:** (l). **54 Chris George:** (bl), (clb). **54-55 Chris George:** (t); **Getty Images:** Panoramic Images (b). **57 Alamy Images:** Rubberball (cra boy); **Corbis:** Stephane Masson (tr). **59 Image Courtesy of Epson:** (crb). **60 Image Courtesy of Epson:** (cl), (tr); **Getty Images:** Nick Pardo (br). **62 Getty:** (cr). **63 Alamy:** (r x4); **Corbis:** David Stoecklein (cla); **Louise Thomas:** (bl).

All other images © Dorling Kindersley.

For further information see:
www.dkimages.com